Great African Americans
Sports

By Jennifer Howse

www.av2books.com

AV² provides enriched content that supplements and complements this book. Weigl's AV² books strive to create inspired learning and engage young minds in a total learning experience.

Your AV² Media Enhanced books come alive with...

Audio
Listen to sections of the book read aloud.

Key Words
Study vocabulary, and complete a matching word activity.

Go to **www.av2books.com**, and enter this book's unique code.

Video
Watch informative video clips.

Quizzes
Test your knowledge.

BOOK CODE

R24749

Embedded Weblinks
Gain additional information for research.

Slide Show
View images and captions, and prepare a presentation.

AV² by Weigl brings you media enhanced books that support active learning.

Try This!
Complete activities and hands-on experiments.

... and much, much more!

Published by AV² by Weigl
350 5th Avenue, 59th Floor
New York, NY 10118

Website: www.weigl.com   www.av2books.com

Library of Congress Cataloging-in-Publication Data

Howse, Jennifer.
 Sports : African American history / Jennifer Howse.
    p. cm. -- (Great African Americans)
 Includes bibliographical references and index.
 ISBN 978-1-61690-660-3 (hardcover : alk. paper) -- ISBN 978-1-61690-664-1 (softcover : alk. paper)
 1. African American athletes--History--Juvenile literature. 2. Sports--United States--History--Juvenile literature. I. Title.
 GV583.H69 2012
 796.08996073--dc22
                              2010050184

Printed in the United States of America in North Mankato, Minnesota
1 2 3 4 5 6 7 8 9 0 15 14 13 12 11

062011
WEP290411

Weigl acknowledges Getty Images as its primary image supplier for this title.

Every reasonable effort has been made to trace ownership and to obtain permission to reprint copyright material. The publishers would be pleased to have any errors or omissions brought to their attention so that they may be corrected in subsequent printings.

Senior Editor: Heather Kissock
Art Director: Terry Paulhus

Contents

Negro
BASEBALL

1946
Yearbook

25¢

★ **Records**

★ **All-America Team**

★ **East-West Game**

★ **World Series**

★ **Crashing the Majors**

Jackie Robinson

Sports and Society

For more than a century, great African American athletes have contributed in a major way to the role of sports in American life. Young people have chosen them as role models and have tried to develop similar skills. People of all ages have cheered for the players who represent their communities.

Athletes Bring Change

The achievements of African American athletes also helped change the way people thought of and acted toward African Americans in general. For most of U.S. history, African Americans were not treated fairly or given equal opportunities. In sports, it was more difficult for African American athletes to compete and show their skills. Over time, however, more African Americans did find ways to take part in major sports. As they did, more Americans saw their athletic talent and leadership skills. This helped reduce **discrimination** against African Americans in many areas of American life. In 1947, for example, when Jackie Robinson became the first African American to play **major league baseball**, some fans and other players shouted insults at him. When his remarkable skills brought a new kind of excitement to baseball, however, he became a national hero. Many people began to view all African Americans in a favorable light.

Henry Aaron was one of the greatest hitters in baseball history. In 1974, he set a new major league record when he hit the 715th home run of his career.

Sports in Africa

Long before they were brought to America as slaves, Africans took part in many sports on their home continent. Athletic skills needed for sports were also part of daily life, and children were encouraged to develop them. For example, children who helped with raising cattle had to become strong runners and jumpers in order to protect the herds. Children were encouraged to learn sporting skills and compete against other children as part of their development. Contests involving the bow and arrow helped sharpen hunting skills. Other sports involved throwing and catching. The passage from childhood into adulthood was marked by achieving a certain skill level or beating an opponent in a race or game.

Sports Competitions

Sports were also a part of adult life. Neighboring groups held competitions that included running, swimming, or climbing races, as well as boat racing. Exceptional athletes were remembered through stories that were told and retold. One of the most ancient forms of sport in Africa is Nuba wrestling. Done by the Nuba people of Sudan, this sport goes back at least 3,000 years. In Nuba wrestling, a competitor tries to throw his opponent to the ground so that he is lying on his back.

Dambe

A type of boxing known as dambe, or sometimes kokawa, originated with the Hausa people of West Africa. Men who made their living as butchers traveled to farm villages to prepare animals for food. As part of

their visit, they would hold a dambe tournament. The butchers would fight each other and then challenge local young men to boxing matches. These matches became part of the harvest celebrations.

In dambe, the fighters use their hands for hitting or grappling and their legs for kicking. Hands are wrapped for protection with cloth held in place by a knotted cord. Legs can be powerful weapons because they are sometimes wrapped with chains. Competitors usually fight an opponent who is a similar size. There are three rounds of fighting. A round ends when one of the fighters or a **referee** stops the fight or when a part of one fighter's body touches the ground. Dambe tournaments are still held in Africa.

Dambe remains popular in the African countries of Nigeria, Niger, and Chad.

Sports in Early America

Despite the oppressive conditions of slavery in the New World, African culture thrived. Although slaves in America had very little time to themselves, different sports and games were played on **plantations** and in towns. Horseshoes, games using marbles, jumping over poles, and walking on stilts were all popular.

African Americans who had been freed from slavery, known as **freedmen**, also took part in sports. Although they were often legally barred from gathering in large groups, they often spent Sundays competing in foot races, ball playing, wrestling, and boxing. One of the ball games was "town ball,"

Quick Facts

Walking races were very popular in the 19th century. Both men and women competed. An African American speed walker named Francis Smith was barred from a race in 1835. The official reason was that he entered the race too late, but the real reason was his skin color.

In the 1850s, African Americans in New Orleans played a game called **raquette**. This game was similar to lacrosse.

Slave owners often held contests in which they would match their slaves against those of other owners. Boxing matches were popular, and large sums were bet on them. A slave named Tom Molineaux won so much money for his owner that he was given his freedom. Molineaux went on to become a **professional** boxer.

or "rounders," which was an early form of baseball. Using a stick with a crook on the end, the player pushed or hit a ball to try to get on base.

During the **colonial period**, African Americans learned to play European games, such as soccer. Generations of African Americans enjoyed sports as a temporary escape from the harsh conditions of their daily lives.

African American boxer Tom Molineaux fought the English champion, Tom Cribb, in 1808. Cribb won, but many thought Molineaux had been cheated of the victory.

The Early Days of Horse Racing

Many of the first professional African American athletes were jockeys. Jockeys are athletes who ride horses in races. Horse racing has long been an important part of American culture. In the southern states, landowners and other wealthy people would organize huge racing events that included parties and gambling. Before the Civil War, the jockeys were often slaves, who were specially trained to race Thoroughbred horses.

The typical slave jockey was a short, thin boy. To hold down his weight, his owner gave him very little to eat. Most slave jockeys would ride horses all morning and then pick crops in the afternoon. The best riders would win a great deal of money for their owners and gain the opportunity to win their freedom.

Champion Jockeys

The best known horse race in the United States is the Kentucky Derby. It was first run in 1875. Fourteen out of the fifteen horses in that first race had African American jockeys. The winning jockey, Oscar Lewis, was an African American. The horse's trainer, Ansel Anderson, was African American as well. Willie Simms was one of the greatest jockeys of the 19th century. He is the only African American jockey to win all three of the U.S. **Triple Crown** races.

Dudley Allen was born into slavery in Kentucky. After gaining his freedom, he became a successful Thoroughbred horse owner and trainer. His horse Kingman won the Kentucky Derby in 1891. Kingman was ridden by Isaac Murphy, who was also an African American.

During his career, Murphy competed in 1,412 races and won 628 of them. His winning percentage of 44 percent is a record that still stands. Isaac Murphy was the first jockey to be inducted into the Museum of Racing and Hall of Fame.

One of jockey Isaac Murphy's greatest wins came when he rode the famous racehorse Salvator to victory at the Sheepshead Bay Race Track in New York in 1890.

Boxing

African American boxing history began when slaves brought their fighting skills to the New World. One of the sport's first stars was an African American named William Richmond, who was the slave of a British general stationed in New York named Earl Percy. Percy brought Richmond to England, where he won several matches against prominent boxers and became known as the "Black Terror." In 1805, Richmond, then 42 years old, lost to the Englishman Tom Cribb, who outweighed Richmond by more than 20 pounds. Two years later, Cribb became the British champion, and Richmond helped train Tom Molineaux when he challenged Cribb for the title. After his retirement from boxing, Richmond ran a boxing school in London.

African American Champions

The late 19th century saw the rise of African American boxing clubs and the development of such professional boxing greats as Joe Gans and Jack Johnson. Many of these fighters had to overcome powerful racial barriers. When Gans won a title in Nevada, racial violence broke out against African Americans across the country in protest.

Gans became lightweight champion in 1902. He was the first African American world title holder in any sport. Even after he became ill with tuberculosis, he defended his title in four more fights.

Joe Gans was known as the "Old Master" because of his boxing skills, quickness in the ring, and tremendous punching power.

Great African American Boxers

From the earliest days of the sport, many of the best boxers in the United States were African American. Three of the best gained their fame in the heavyweight division.

Jack Johnson (1878–1946)

Jack Johnson was the first African American to win the world heavyweight championship. During his professional career, which lasted from 1897 to 1928, he fought more than 100 fights and won more than 70. He captured the heavyweight crown by defeating Canada's Tommy Burns in 1908. Johnson defended the title many times before losing to Jess Willard in 1915. While he was champion, some people who opposed having an African American title holder wanted a "Great White Hope" to defeat him.

Joe Louis (1914–1981)

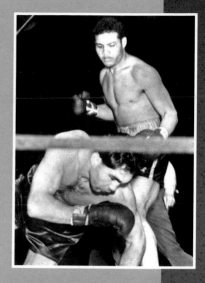

Known as the "Brown Bomber," Louis fought 68 fights during his career and lost only three. His first loss came in 1936 at the hands of a German fighter named Max Schmeling. The Nazis, who were in power in Germany, considered Schmeling's victory to be proof of German racial superiority. However, in a rematch in 1938, Louis knocked out Schmeling in the first round. The victory made Louis an instant American hero. He held the heavyweight championship for almost 12 years, a record that still stands.

Muhammad Ali (1942–)

Cassius Marcellus Clay, Jr., was born in Louisville, Kentucky. He decided to become a boxer at the age of 12. At the 1960 **Olympic Games**, Clay won the light heavyweight **gold medal** and then turned professional as a heavyweight. He won the championship in 1964 by beating Sonny Liston. In that year, he converted to **Islam** and changed his name to Muhammad Ali. Known as "The Greatest," Ali described his fighting style as "float like a butterfly and sting like a bee." In 1999, *Sports Illustrated* named him "Sportsman of the Century."

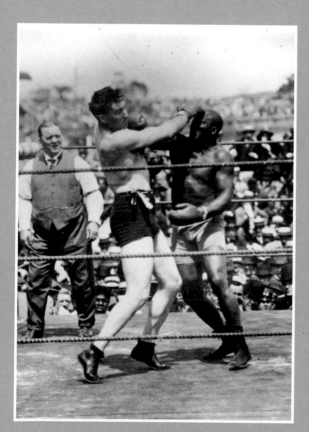

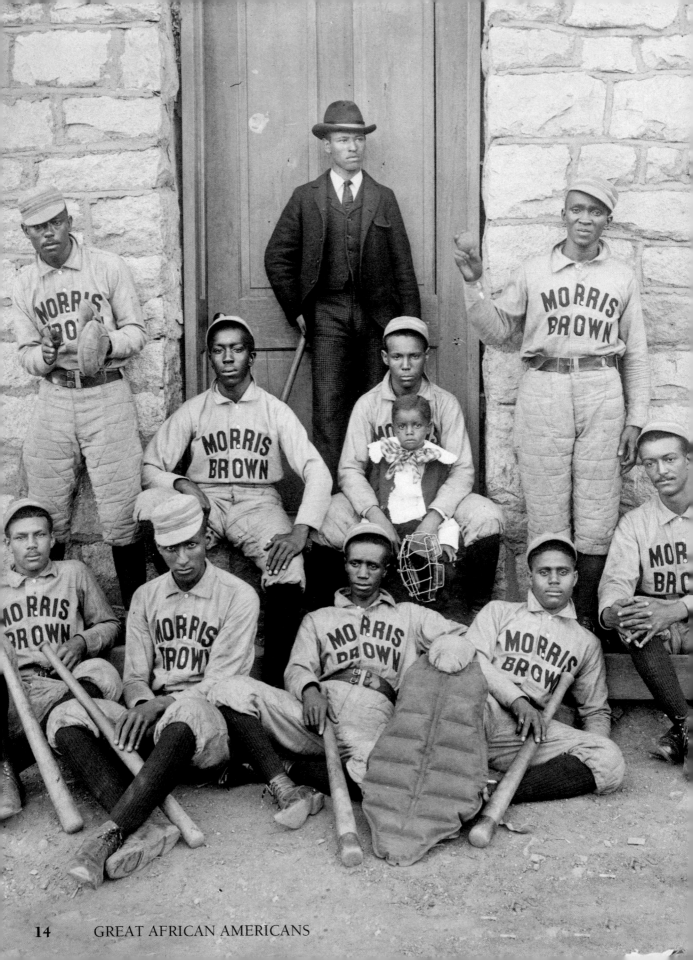

Sports After the Civil War

The Civil War brought the emancipation of the slaves and new opportunities for African Americans. During the war, southern race tracks were closed, and many African American jockeys who were able to reach the North moved there. After the war, African American men and women began to take part in a great variety of sporting activities that were popular at the time, including town ball, tennis, and bowling. However, many African American athletes were not permitted to join athletic clubs except for those established just for African Americans.

Even before the Civil War, the Young Men's Christian Association, or YMCA, had begun to establish separate facilities for African Americans. After emancipation, access increased to YMCA athletic clubs. In these clubs, African Americans were able to participate in organized sports in large numbers.

College Sports

After the Civil War, U.S. colleges and universities began developing major sports programs. African American institutions did so too. The Ashmun Institute, later renamed Lincoln University, established baseball and football teams. Other African American schools, such as the institution now called Tuskegee University, also had sport teams that competed in **varsity** matches. In addition, after studying sports education, young African Americans returned to their communities and coached sports in schools and clubs.

The first football game between two African American colleges took place in 1892. As more than 10,000 fans watched, the Golden Bulls of Biddle University defeated the Blue Bears of Livingstone College.

Oberlin College, founded in 1883, was a **co-educational** college that accepted students of all races, including African Americans. Moses Fleetwood Walker was an African American student at Oberlin who was a catcher on the school's varsity baseball team. Walker went on to play professional baseball.

In the 1880s, many African Americans began appearing on football teams at colleges that accepted students of all races. In 1889, Thomas Fisher played for Beloit College. William Henry Lewis played football at Amherst College in 1889. He was the first African American player to become an **All-American**. After graduating from Amherst, Lewis went on to Harvard Law School. For the next two years, he played center on the Harvard football team.

Baseball

Early forms of baseball were popular in the United States even before the Civil War. After the war, however, baseball spread across the country and became the most popular game in the nation. At first, it was played by **amateurs** who formed their own teams and leagues. Leading African American amateur teams included the Brooklyn Uniques, Philadelphia Excelsiors, and Brooklyn Monitors, who won the first African American championship series in 1867. In that same year, a Boston "Negro Championship" was played.

The first organization to oversee baseball in the United States was the National Association of Baseball Players, which was created in 1857.

In 1867 the association denied membership to an African American team called the Philadelphia Pythians. Baseball had established its first "color line."

Professional baseball began in 1871 with the creation of the National Association of Professional Baseball Players, which had nine teams. The National League replaced it in 1876. At first, the National League did not bar African American players. Some players, however, refused to play against teams that included African Americans. Gradually, African American players were kept out of professional baseball. There was no written rule barring them, but the owners of the teams in the National League agreed among themselves not to hire African American players. The same thing happened in the American League after it was formed in 1901.

African Americans had to form their own, separate professional teams. What is considered the "Golden Age" of African American professional baseball began in 1920 with the creation of the Negro National League. Some of the greatest baseball players of all time played in this popular league. It went out of business in 1948, the year after major league baseball began to include African American players.

TECHNOLOGY LINK
To find out more about Negro National League baseball, visit **www.negroleaguebaseball.com**.

Diamond Dazzlers

Whether they played in the Negro National League or in the major leagues, many African Americans were outstanding baseball players in the 20th century.

Leroy "Satchel" Paige (1906–1982)
Paige spent 22 years in the Negro National League as its finest pitcher. At one point, he pitched 64 consecutive scoreless innings and won 21 straight games. In 1933 his record was 31–4. He struck out many major leaguers in exhibition games, proving that he was one of the greatest pitchers of all time. In 1948, he signed with the Cleveland Indians, becoming one of the oldest rookies in major league baseball history.

Jackie Robinson (1919–1972)
In college, Robinson starred in baseball, basketball, football, and track at the University of California, Los Angeles, or UCLA. In 1945, he signed with the Brooklyn Dodgers. Two years later, he became the first African American to play in a major league baseball game. Robinson earned the National League's Rookie of the Year award in 1947. Two years later, he won the **Most Valuable Player** award in the National League. In 1962, he was inducted into the Baseball Hall of Fame.

Henry "Hank" Aaron (1934–)
Aaron began his career in the Negro National League. He came to the major leagues in 1954 with the Milwaukee Braves. During his career,

he had 3,771 hits and a lifetime batting average of .305. His most famous achievement was breaking Babe Ruth's lifetime home run record of 714. Aaron hit a total of 755 home runs. He entered the Hall of Fame in 1982.

Jim Crow Laws

The **Jim Crow laws** were state and local laws passed in many southern states in the late 1800s. They separated people based upon skin color. For example, some Jim Crow laws required the **segregation** of public schools, restaurants and other public places, buses and other kinds of transportation, restrooms, and even such things as water fountains. The first Jim Crow law was passed in Tennessee in the 1860s.

A Supreme Court Ruling

Many people did not like the Jim Crow laws and believed they were extremely unfair to African Americans. However, in 1896, the U.S. Supreme Court decided a case known as *Plessy v. Ferguson*. In this case, the court ruled that segregation was permitted under the United States Constitution as long as the separate facilities were equal. Often, separate schools, playgrounds, and other facilities for African Americans were inferior rather than equal. This was very hard to prove, though. As a result, the Supreme Court decision allowed legal segregation to continue for more than half a century. Only in 1954 was the Plessy decision overturned in another Supreme Court case, *Brown v. Board of Education*.

Segregation and Sports

Although sports or recreation activities were sometimes not specifically addressed in the Jim Crow laws, segregation was widespread from the 1890s to 1940s. Public events such as baseball games often had spectators' sections marked "White Only" and "Colored Only." African American jockeys were refused the licenses they needed in order to race. Some colleges had quotas for how many African American players could be on football teams. Many professional boxers, including John L. Sullivan, who was the heavyweight champion from 1885 until 1892, would not fight African American challengers. African American players were not allowed to play at some tennis courts.

Some Jim Crow laws passed in individual states could be very detailed. For example, in Georgia, it was "unlawful for any amateur colored baseball team to play baseball in any vacant lot or baseball diamond within two blocks of any playground devoted to the white race." In Oklahoma, a law was passed that "the baths and lockers for the Negroes shall be separate from the white race, but may be in the same building." African American athletes were made to feel unwanted by many people in American society

Track and Field

Track and field sports began to become popular in the United States after the Civil War. Most athletes competed either as members of athletic clubs or on college track teams. The New York Athletic Club was formed in 1868 and held its first national competition in 1876. The Intercollegiate Association of Amateur Athletes of America organized college races in 1873, and in 1888, the Amateur Athletic Union held its first championships. African Americans usually were not able to become members of athletic clubs, unless they formed their own.

Many, however, did train at African American colleges. These colleges organized special days for the schools' athletes to compete with one another.

Tuskegee Institute, a well-known African American college that is now Tuskegee University, hired its first sports director, James B. Washington, in 1890. He built the school's sports program and organized its first track meet, which was held in 1896. The meet included running and jumping events, as well as throwing weights and tug of war.

Charles Dumas made history in 1956 by becoming the first person to high jump 7 feet (2.1 meters), an achievement once considered impossible.

Outstanding Competitors

Some early African American track stars competed at colleges that accepted students of all races. One such star was William Tecumseh Sherman Jackson, who graduated from Amherst College in 1893. He competed in the half-mile race, as well as being a star football player. Jackson went on to coach sports and teach mathematics at a high school in Washington, D.C.

Another well-known African American track athlete was Napoleon Bonaparte Marshall, who raced for Harvard University's track team in the 1890s. His specialty was the 440-yard race. In 1897, he finished third at the intercollegiate track championships in New York. His best time for the 440-yard dash was 51.2 seconds. Marshall became a prominent New York attorney and served as a soldier in World War I.

Theodore "Ted" Cable was another African American track and field athlete at Harvard University. He competed on the relay team, in the hammer throw, and in the long jump. In 1912, he won the hammer throw event in a competition against Yale University, a traditional rival of Harvard's.

Howard Porter Drew, who competed for the University of Southern California from 1913 to 1916, held several world records in sprint races. He was the first person to run the 100-yard dash in under 10 seconds. He was called the "world's fastest human."

Today, both men and women compete in track and field events. Since those early days, African American athletes have broken many world records. They have also won medals and set records in the Olympic Games.

Bob Beamon shattered the world long jump record at the Mexico City Olympics in 1968. His mark of 29 feet 2.5 inches (8.9 meters) remained the record for 23 years.

Women Find a Way to Compete

After the Civil War, a great many American women began to express their desire to participate in sports as men did. African American women were part of this movement. In the era of Jim Crow laws, African American women established their own sporting clubs. One of these clubs was the Spartan Athletic Club. It started in 1910 in Brooklyn, New York. This club had a successful basketball team and also offered track and field sports to its members. Another club, the New York Girls, started in 1909.

Track and field was very popular with African American women, and universities such as Tuskegee Institute and Tennessee State University had women's teams. Between 1937 and 1950, the Tuskegee women's track team won 14 National Amateur Athletic Union outdoor track team championships. More recently, in the 1950s and 1960s, Tennessee State University had some outstanding athletes on its women's track team. Members of the Tigerbelles track team captured 34 Amateur Athletic Union titles.

African American Lusia Harris was a star on the Delta State University women's basketball team before competing in the 1976 Olympic Games.

Fifteen of those competitors went on to win Olympic gold medals.

Basketball Stars

Basketball has attracted top African American women athletes. In 1976, Lusia Harris played on the U.S. Olympic basketball team. After the Olympics, she was drafted by the New Orleans Jazz of the National Basketball Association, although she decided not to join the team. In the 1980s, Cheryl Miller became one of the most highly regarded high school and collegiate women's basketball players in history. As a high school player, she once scored 105 points in a game. Miller led the University of Southern California women's team to the national championship twice. She then led the U.S. women's basketball team to a gold medal in the 1984 Olympics.

Quick Facts

Two African American women's basketball teams were founded in the 1930s. The Chicago Romas and the Philadelphia Tribune played tournaments throughout the American Midwest. The Romas played against both men's and women's teams and did not lose a game for six years.

Cynthia Cooper was one of the pioneers of the Women's National Basketball Association, or WNBA. In 1997, she led the Houston Comets to victory in the WNBA's first championship tournament. Her team then went on to capture the next three championships. She was the first WNBA player to score 2,500 points in her career.

Cheryl Miller scored more than 3,000 points during her college career at the University of Southern California.

Olympic Stars

The summer Olympic Games are held every four years. The best athletes in the world compete. Many African Americans have won medals at the Olympics.

The first African American to win an Olympic medal was George Coleman Poage at the 1904 games in St. Louis, Missouri. A graduate of the University of Wisconsin, Poage won the bronze medal in both the 200-meter and the 400-meter hurdles. The first African American to win a gold medal was John Baxter Taylor, Jr. He was a member of the U.S. 4 x 400-meter relay team at the London Olympics in 1908. Alice Coachman, who won the high jump at the 1948 games, was the first African American woman to win an Olympic gold medal.

Historic Performance

Perhaps the most memorable Olympic performance by an African American came in 1936, when the Olympic Games were held in Berlin, Germany. The Nazi regime was in power, and its leader, Adolf Hitler, wanted to showcase German superiority. However, an African American athlete named Jesse Owens ruined Hitler's plan. Owens won the 100-meter race by setting a new record of 10.3 seconds. He also won the 200-meter race with a time of 20.7 seconds, another world record. Owens won the long jump with a leap of 26.4 feet (8.06 meters), and he won a fourth gold medal in the 4 x 100-meter relay.

Alice Coachman set an Olympic record in the high jump when she cleared 5' 6 1/8" (1.68 meters) at the 1948 Olympics in London.

The Fastest and Strongest

Every four years, the talents of African American athletes are on display at the Olympic Games. Some of their performances have been especially remarkable.

Jesse Owens (1913–1980)

After starring in track in high school, Owens went to Ohio State University. At a college championship meet in 1935, he set a world record in the long jump that was not broken for 25 years. In addition to winning four gold medals at the 1936 Olympic Games, Owens held or shared the world records for all the sprint distances. In 1976, he received the Presidential Medal of Freedom.

Wilma Rudolph (1940–1994)

Wilma Rudolph qualified for the 1956 U.S.

Olympic team while still in high school. She was 16 when she competed in the Olympics in Melbourne, Australia. At the 1960 games in Rome, Italy, Rudolph won gold medals in the 100-meter, 200-meter, and sprint relay events. She became the first American woman to win three gold medals at a single Olympic games.

Carl Lewis (1961–)

Both of Lewis's parents were star athletes. He attended the University of Houston, where he began his training for the Olympics. During his career, Lewis won nine Olympic gold medals. At the 1984 games in Los Angeles, Lewis matched Jesse Owens's feat of winning four gold medals at a single Olympics. *Sports Illustrated* magazine named Lewis "Olympian of the Century."

Florence Griffith-Joyner (1959–1998)

Nicknamed "Flo Jo," Griffith-Joyner won three gold medals at the 1988 Olympics in Seoul, South Korea. An outstanding sprinter, she was victorious in the 100-meter race, the 200-meter race, and the 4 x 100-meter relay. After retiring from track, she served as co-chair of the President's Council on Physical Fitness and Sports.

Basketball

Basketball was invented in 1891 by a physical education teacher named James Naismith. Since its earliest days, many African Americans have starred in the sport. One of the first of these players was Harry Bucky Lew. He joined the Pawtucket Athletic Club in 1902 and played forward. Lew was paid five dollars, making him the first African American to become a professional basketball player.

Early NBA Stars

The first African American professional players entered the National Basketball Association, or NBA, in 1950. The first African American to be selected in the NBA draft was Chuck Cooper, who was chosen by the Boston Celtics. The first African American to actually play in an NBA game was Earl Lloyd, who made his debut with the Washington Capitols on October 31, 1950. Lloyd reported that he was accepted without any problems by his teammates. Some spectators, however, were slow to accept him. During a game in Fort Wayne, Indiana, for example, several fans spit on Lloyd.

Forward Earl Lloyd played college ball at West Virginia State University before playing professionally in the National Basketball Association.

TECHNOLOGY LINK
To find out more about the events and people that shaped professional basketball, visit **www.nba.com**.

They Called Him "Wilt the Stilt"

Wilt Chamberlain was one of the most talented basketball players of all time. Born in Philadelphia, Pennsylvania, he started playing basketball at Overbrook High School. Chamberlain played college ball for the University of Kansas. There he developed many of the skills that made him an outstanding player, including his great shot blocking.

Standing 7′ 1″ (2.1 meters) tall and nicknamed "Wilt the Stilt," he was a dominant force on both offense and defense. In his first NBA season, he was named both Most Valuable Player and Rookie of the Year. On March 2, 1962, he scored 100 points in a game, a record that still stands. He ended his NBA career with a total of 31,419 points scored.

Stars of the Court

African American basketball stars have often achieved impressive statistics during their careers. Many of them have also led their teams to one or more championships.

The player who holds the NBA record for scoring the most points during his years in the league is Kareem Abdul-Jabbar. By the time he retired as a player in 1989, Abdul-Jabbar had a career total of 38,387 points. Born Ferdinand Lewis "Lew" Alcindor, Jr., he played high school basketball in New York City. He helped his high school team win 71 consecutive games. When he converted to Islam, he changed his name to Kareem Abdul-Jabbar. In college, Abdul-Jabbar led UCLA to three national championships in the 1960s. After starting his professional career in 1969, he was a member of six NBA championship teams. He was also named the Most Valuable Player in the NBA six times.

Greatest Player of All Time

The person who is often called the greatest basketball player of all time is Michael Jordan. Born in Brooklyn, New York, Jordan played college ball at the University of North Carolina, or UNC. His game-winning shot in the championship game helped UNC with the national title in 1982.

Kareem Abdul-Jabbar was famous for his high, arching "sky hook" shot. It is an almost impossible shot for a defensive player to block.

Jordan went on to lead the Chicago Bulls to six NBA championships in the 1990s, and he was named the NBA's Most Valuable Player five times. A great scorer, Jordan was also famous for his defensive skills.

Sheryl Swoopes

Born in Brownfield, Texas, in 1971, Sheryl Swoopes was one of the greatest players in the history of the Women's National Basketball Association, or WNBA. As a college player, she led Texas Tech to a national championship in 1993. During her professional career, Swoopes helped the Houston Comets win four straight WNBA championships from 1997 to 2000. She was named Most Valuable Player three times. Swoopes also played on the U.S. Olympic teams that won gold medals in 1996, 2000, and 2004. She is the first woman to have a Nike basketball shoe named after her. It is called the "Air Swoopes."

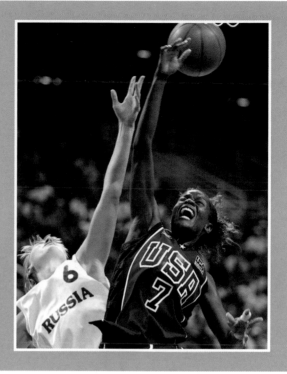

Michael Jordan was also known as "Air Jordan" because he seemed able to "hang" in the air for a long time when he jumped.

Quick Facts

In 1966, the men's basketball team at Texas Western College, now known as the University of Texas at El Paso, became the first college team to start five African American players in the National Collegiate Athletic Association, or NCAA, championship game. The team's victory over Kentucky was a milestone in African American sports history.

The first African American to coach a major college basketball program was Will Robinson, who took over at Illinois State in 1970.

Football

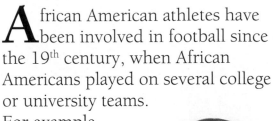

African American athletes have been involved in football since the 19th century, when African Americans played on several college or university teams. For example, William Henry Lewis played for Amherst College, where he was elected team captain.

Another early African American football star was Paul Robeson, who played for Rutgers and was named an All-American in 1917 and 1918. He played the position of end on the team. Robeson faced racial discrimination throughout his college career. Some schools in the South would not play against Rutgers because he was on the team. Robeson did play against schools such as Columbia University in New York City. The coach of Columbia's football team considered Robeson the best football player he had ever seen. After college, Robeson played professional football for the Akron Pros and

Paul Robeson was not only a football star at Rutgers University. He competed in baseball, basketball, and track as well. He was a brilliant student who ranked first in his class.

Milwaukee Badgers. He then went on to become a renowned singer, actor, and civil rights leader.

Early Professional Players

Frederick Douglass "Fritz" Pollard was another talented African American player of the early 1900s. He starred first at Brown University and then with the Akron Pros. When he became head coach of the Pros in 1921, he was the first African American head coach in the National Football League, or NFL.

Ray Kemp was one of the earliest African American professional football players. He faced a great deal of racial discrimination. After college, he played for the J.P. Rooneys, which became the Pittsburgh Pirates and later the Pittsburgh Steelers. On at least one occasion when the team was playing on the road, Kemp was not permitted to stay in the same hotel as the rest of the team. Instead, he was asked to sleep at a YMCA in an African American neighborhood. Kemp played only three games for the Pirates in 1933 before he was cut from the roster, apparently because of the coach's opposition to having Kemp on the team. Kemp was called up to play one more game against the New York Giants late in the season. After his short stay in the NFL, he enjoyed a long college coaching career.

Jim Brown

Born in 1936, Jim Brown was a great athlete from a young age. He earned 13 letters for lacrosse, basketball, baseball, track, and football at Manhasset Secondary School in Manhasset, New York. After attending Syracuse University, he entered the NFL in 1956 as a first-round draft pick of the Cleveland Browns. He led the NFL in rushing for eight of his nine seasons in the league. He averaged 5.2 yards per carry during his career, which is still the NFL record.

Football Stars and Leaders

As Ray Kemp's career shows, some African Americans faced difficulties but did play in the NFL in its early days. From 1934 to 1946, however, African Americans were not admitted into the NFL. Then, the emergence of a rival league called the All-American Football Conference, or AAFC, prompted NFL team owners to revoke the ban.

It was the Cleveland Browns of the AAFC who signed the first African American professional football players since 1933. Marion Motley and Bill Willis both joined Cleveland in 1946. Motley, a running back, gained more than 3,000 yards (2,750 meters) in his four years in the AAFC. With him on the team, the Cleveland Browns lost only four games. Willis starred as a defensive guard who was famous for his speed and for his hard-hitting tackles.

Owners of NFL teams soon realized they would have to sign African American players themselves before all the best ones ended up in the AAFC. Integration of the NFL was slow, however, and **civil rights** groups put pressure on NFL teams to sign more African American players. The last NFL team to have no African American players was the Washington Redskins, until Washington acquired Bobby Mitchell in 1962.

African American Quarterbacks

African Americans found it especially difficult to become professional quarterbacks. The quarterback is a team's on-the-field leader. In the past, some players did not want to be led by an African American. Also, some people unfairly believed that African Americans would not make good leaders. These attitudes and ideas resulted in discrimination that was not easy to overcome.

The first African American quarterback to play in an NFL game was Willie Thrower, who appeared in just one game for the Chicago Bears in 1953. It was 15 years later when the second African American quarterback, Marlin Briscoe, played for the Denver Broncos. Since then, however, many African American quarterbacks have starred in the NFL. Some of the best have been Warren Moon, Randall

Quick Facts

The first known African American professional football player was Charles Follis. He played for the Shelby Athletic Club of Shelby, Ohio, from 1902 to 1905.

The first African American head coach to win a **Super Bowl** was Tony Dungy, who led the Indianapolis Colts to victory in 2007.

Walter Payton

Payton was born in Columbia, Mississippi, in 1954. At Jackson State University in Mississippi, he was named Black College Player of the Year in 1973 and 1974. Starting in 1975, he was a running back for the Chicago Bears of the NFL for 13 seasons. With the Bears, he ran for 6,726 yards (6,150 meters) and scored 125 touchdowns. One of his specialties was leaping over a wall of defenders to score a touchdown. Payton also missed only one game in his entire career. That is very unusual in the NFL, where injuries are common.

Cunningham, Steve McNair, and Donovan McNabb.

In 1988, Doug Williams of the Washington Redskins became the first African American quarterback to lead his team to victory in the Super Bowl. Williams completed 18 of 29 passes for 340 yards (310 meters) and four touchdowns. He was named the game's Most Valuable Player.

African American Coaches

African Americans have moved into head coaching positions with professional football teams. In recent decades, the first African American to become head coach of an NFL team was Art Shell, who took over the Los Angeles Raiders in 1989. Other notable African American NFL head coaches include Herm Edwards of the New York Jets, Mike Tomlin of the Pittsburgh Steelers, Romeo Crennel of the Cleveland Browns, Tony Dungy of the Indianapolis Colts, and Lovie Smith of the Chicago Bears.

TECHNOLOGY LINK
To find out more about the records of African American football stars, visit www.nfl.com.

Golf

Golf became popular in the United States in the second half of the 19th century, but gaining access to golf courses and country clubs was difficult for African Americans and other minorities. Barred from playing as competitors, African Americans worked at the courses as **caddies** and groundskeepers. Working as caddies is how many African American golfers gained their start and developed their skills in the game. Some African American golfers also organized leagues for themselves.

An African American golfer named John Shippen played in six U.S. Opens in the early 20th century. He was able to play because his mother was a Shinnecock Indian. Shippen entered the tournament as an Indian player. At Shippen's first Open, the other golfers found out that Shippen's father was African American and threatened to withdraw. However, the president of the U.S. Golf Association insisted that the tournament continue. Officially, African Americans were not allowed to compete in professional golf until 1961.

Lee Elder played in the Masters tournament in 1975 and 1977.

Pioneering Professionals

The first African American to become a full-time professional golfer was Charlie Sifford. He joined the pro tour in 1961, when he was 39 years old. In 2004, Sifford became the first African American to enter the World Golf Hall of Fame.

In the 1970s, Lee Elder was the first African American to play in the Masters tournament, which is considered golf's top championship. Elder faced a great deal of hostility. He sometimes needed police to escort him around the golf course during tournaments because he had received threats.

What Lee Elder was to men's golf, Ann Moore-Gregory was to women's golf. Born in Aberdeen, Mississippi, in 1912, she began playing golf in the 1940s. In 1956, she was the first African American to play in the U.S. Women's Amateur Championship. Moore-Gregory golfed for more than 50 years. During that time, she won more than 300 tournaments.

Tiger Woods

Born in Cypress, California, in 1975, Woods learned the game of golf from his father. Woods attended Stanford University and won many amateur golf tournaments before turning professional in 1996. At his first Masters tournament, in 1997, he won by 12 strokes. Winning by such a large margin is extremely rare in major professional golf tournaments. Woods also shot a record score of 270. During his career, his many tournament victories have led many people to call Woods one of the greatest golfers of all time.

Tennis

Tennis originated in Europe and was brought to the United States during the colonial period. The United States Tennis Association, or USTA, which was founded in 1881, at first did not permit African Americans to join. African American players formed their own organization, called the American Tennis Association, or ATA. The ATA sponsored tournaments across the country.

A tennis star since high school, Althea Gibson won several major tournaments in her career. She titled her autobiography *I Always Wanted to Be Somebody.*

Early Stars

In 1914, Florence Brooks, one of the ATA's early stars, won an ATA tournament at the Chautauqua Club. Anita Ganntt was another great African American tennis players in the first half of the 20th century. She won the ATA women's singles title in 1925 and 1926. Margaret and Roumania Peters dominated the doubles event for years, winning championships from 1938 to 1953.

One of the finest African American players was Ora Washington. She won her first ATA singles title in 1929 and then when on to win six more in a row. She wanted to challenge Helen Wills Moody, the top women's player in the USTA, but segregation laws and discrimination kept the match from being played.

African American Champions

By the second half of the 20th century, African American tennis professionals gained greater opportunities to compete. The first African American woman to gain admission to the USTA was Althea Gibson. Gibson won the French Open in 1956. She went on to win at Wimbledon and at the U.S. Open in both 1957 and 1958. She was the first African American, man or woman, to win a major tennis tournament.

After his tennis career ended, Arthur Ashe wrote a three-volume history of African American athletes.

One of the greatest stars of the 1960s and 1970s was Arthur Ashe. He attended the University of California, and in 1963 he became the first African American to play on the U.S. **Davis Cup** team. He won the U.S. Open in 1968 and then went on to win the Australian Open in 1970 and the Wimbledon tournament in 1975.

Venus and Serena Williams

Beginning in the late 1990s, the Williams sisters of California became two of the most dominant players in women's tennis. Venus was born in 1980 and Serena in 1981. Coached by their father, they showed their talents at an early age. Venus won the very first tournament she entered, and both sisters turned professional at age 14. Serena won her first major championship, the U.S. Open, in 1999, and Venus's first major championship came a year later at Wimbledon. At different times, both Venus and Serena have been ranked number one in the world. The Williams sisters have often played against each other in the singles finals of a major tournament. They also play together in doubles matches.

Former ESPN broadcaster Robin Roberts became co-host of ABC's *Good Morning America* in 2005. She interviewed many guests on the program, including champion race car driver Jimmie Johnson.

Sports and Television

Television changed sports in a major way. In the 1950s and 1960s, sporting events began being broadcast to millions across the country. Athletes became TV stars, and a growing number of them were African American.

These new TV stars were important in the African American community. As the last of the Jim Crow laws were struck down, African American youths were looking for new identities. Segregation was being challenged, and sports became a public playing field where issues of racism and equality could be confronted. New stars on the playing field were looked to as role models.

At the same time, athletes who challenged and crossed the color line, such as Jackie Robinson and Lee Elder, were themselves challenged by public scrutiny. Robinson, for example, was grateful for his family's support, which helped him cope with the pressure of being in the public eye.

In the age of television, one of the new challenges for African Americans has been the broadcasting booth. In TV's early days, many former athletes were hired to cover sports on television, but none were African American. Eventually, retired African American athletes were given broadcasting jobs. The first African American to work as a sports broadcaster on national television was former football player Irv Cross, who joined CBS Sports in 1971.

After an outstanding professional football career as a wide receiver, Ahmad Rashad became a sports broadcaster.

Among those who have followed him are baseball player Joe Morgan, football stars Ahmad Rashad, Lynn Swann, and Michael Strahan, and basketball players Bill Russell, Quinn Buckner, and Reggie Miller. Robin Roberts, who played on the women's basketball team at Southeastern Louisiana University, was a broadcaster with the ESPN sports network for 15 years beginning in 1990. While she was at ESPN, she won three Emmy Awards. She left ESPN to join ABC-TV News.

Former baseball All-Star Joe Morgan has announced games and conducted on-field interviews for ABC Sports, NBC Sports, and ESPN.

Looking to the Future

As opportunities for African Americans have generally increased in U.S. society, African American athletes have begun taking part in many different kinds of sports in which they have not traditionally played a major role.

For example, African American athletes have increasingly taken up winter sports. Debi Thomas won the World Figure Skating Championships in 1986 and a bronze medal at the 1988 Olympics. She is the only African American to ever win a medal in Olympic figure skating. Shani Davis, a speed skater, won Olympic gold medals in both 2006 and 2010. There are also increasing numbers of African American skiers and snowboarders. Several players of African American descent have played in the National

After her very successful skating career, Debi Thomas returned to school and became a doctor.

Hockey League, or NHL, in recent years.

In 1961, Wendell Scott became the first African American race car driver to join the National Association for Stock Car Auto Racing, or NASCAR, circuit. He drove in nearly 500 races during his career and finished first in a race at Speedway Park in Jacksonville, Florida, in 1963. In 2010, Tia Norfleet became the first African American woman NASCAR driver.

Perhaps even more important, greater numbers of African Americans have become coaches, managers, and team owners. For example, Michael Jordan became a part owner of the Charlotte Bobcats professional basketball team in 2006. As opportunities for African Americans have expanded in so many areas of American life, they will continue to widen in sports as well.

At the 2010 Winter Olympics, Shani Davis became the first speed skater to repeat as champion in the 1,000-meter race.

Wendell Scott competed in the NASCAR circuit for more than 40 years.

Timeline

1619: Africans are captured and brought to Jamestown, Virginia, to work as slaves.

1619

1807: Congress declares it illegal to bring slaves into the United States.

1810: African American boxer Tom Molineaux fights British champion Tom Cribb. It is the first major international match fought by an African American boxer.

1835: African American speed walker Francis Smith is barred from competing in a race because of his color.

1861: The Civil War begins.

1863: President Abraham Lincoln issues the Emancipation Proclamation.

1863

1875: The first Kentucky Derby is run. Fourteen out of the fifteen horses are ridden by African American jockeys.

1889: African American players appear on college football teams. William Henry Lewis plays for Harvard University and Thomas Fischer plays for Beloit College.

1896: In *Plessy v. Ferguson*, the U.S. Supreme Court rules that segregation is constitutional as long as the separate facilities are equal.

1896: John Shippen, an African American golfer, plays in the U.S. open.

1896: Under the direction of James B. Washington, Tuskegee Institute, a well-known African American college, holds its first track meet.

1902: Lightweight fighter Joe Gans becomes the first African American to win a world title in boxing.

1910: Jack Johnson knocks out Jim Jeffries and becomes the first African American to officially win the heavyweight boxing championship.

1910

1920: The Negro National League is formed for African American baseball players.

1600   1800   1870   1900

1927: Frederick Douglass "Fritz" Pollard becomes the first African American head coach in the National Football League.

1936: The Olympic Games are held in Berlin. Jesse Owens wins four gold medals.

1936

1938: Two years after losing to German fighter Max Schmeling, heavyweight boxer Joe Louis defeats Schmeling in a rematch, knocking him out in one round.

1947: Playing for the Brooklyn Dodgers, Jackie Robinson breaks baseball's "color barrier" and becomes the first African American athlete on a major league team.

1947

1948: Alice Coachman wins the high jump at the 1948 Olympic Games, becoming the first African American woman to win an Olympic gold medal.

1957: Althea Gibson wins at Wimbledon and becomes the first African American to win a major tennis tournament.

1968: Arthur Ashe wins the U.S. Open tennis championship.

1975: Lee Elder becomes the first African American golfer to play in the Masters tournament.

1975

1976: Lusia Harris plays on the Olympic basketball team. After the Olympics, she is drafted by the New Orleans Jazz of the National Basketball Association.

1992: Led by Michael Jordan and other African American athletes, the U.S. basketball team wins a gold medal at the Olympic Games. The players are known as the "Dream Team."

1997: Tiger Woods competes in his first Masters tournament and wins by 12 strokes, shooting a record score of 270.

2009: Serena Williams defeats her sister Venus to win the Wimbledon women's singles title. The match is just one of many times the two tennis stars play each other in a tournament final.

2010: Speed skater Shani Davis wins the 1,000-meter race at the Winter Olympics for the second consecutive time.

1930   1960   1990   2010

Activity

Inventing a Sport

In 1834, Robin Carver wrote *The Book of Sports*, which describes the types of sporting activities that were popular at that time. Included in the book are rules for sports and games. These games and sporting activities were often played by African American athletes.

Imagine that you are a coach and would like to create a new game in which players could develop physical skills, work as a team, and compete to win. Think about where the game would be played, how the game would be played, what roles different team members would have, and how a winner would be decided.

Decide if the players need any equipment, such as a racquet or stick. Figure out how many players should be on each team and what kind of contribution each position on the team should make. Decide how long the game lasts, and make a list of rules. Test the game by describing it to somebody else or actually playing it. You might start a new sport!

You will need:

✓ a pen
✓ paper
✓ access to the Internet

Test Your Knowledge

Q What was the traditional occupation of the men who took part in dambe?

A Butcher

Q How many gold medals did Wilma Rudolph win at the 1960 Olympic Games in Rome?

A Three

Q How many horses were ridden by African American jockeys at the first running of the Kentucky Derby?

A 14

Q In what year did baseball's Negro National League begin play?

A 1920

Q Who was the heavyweight boxer who knocked out Max Schmeling of Germany in 1938?

A Joe Louis

Q Who was the first African American head coach to win a Super Bowl?

A Tony Dungy

Glossary

All-American: an honor given to outstanding college athletes, most notably in football, but also in other sports

amateurs: people who take part in a sport or other activity for fun and not for pay

caddies: people who assist golfers by carrying clubs and giving advice

civil rights: freedoms and the right to equal treatment that all Americans are entitled to but that were denied to many African Americans for much of U.S. history

co-educational: a school that admits both men and women

colonial period: the time in U.S. history before the Revolutionary War

Davis Cup: the trophy that is awarded to the tennis team that wins a famous yearly international tennis competition

discrimination: unfair treatment because of a person's race, heritage, or other characteristic

emancipation: the act of freeing people from slavery

freedmen: people who have been freed from slavery

gold medal: the top prize in a sports competition, such as an Olympic event

Islam: the religion of Muslim people, started by Muhammad in the 600s

Jim Crow laws: state and local laws that separated people and communities based upon skin color

major league baseball: the highest level of professional baseball in North America, consisting of the National League and the American League

most valuable player: a person who is voted the best player in a sports league

Olympic Games: sporting competitions that started in ancient Greece and that are now held every four years

plantation: in the American South before the Civil War, a large farm on which slaves were used to grow and harvest the crops

professional: in sports, an athlete who is paid to play

raquette: a game similar to lacrosse that was played in the 1850s by African Americans in New Orleans

referee: an official who ensures that the rules of a game are followed correctly

segregation: a forced separation of people based on skin color or race

Super Bowl: a yearly game that decides who is the champion of the National Football League

Triple Crown: the three classic horse races in the United States, which are the Kentucky Derby, the Preakness Stakes, and the Belmont Stakes

varsity: the highest level of team play at a high school, college, or university

Index

Log on to www.av2books.com

AV² by Weigl brings you media enhanced books that support active learning. Go to www.av2books.com, and enter the special code found on page 2 of this book. You will gain access to enriched and enhanced content that supplements and complements this book. Content includes video, audio, web links, quizzes, a slide show, and activities.

Audio
Listen to sections of the book read aloud.

Video
Watch informative video clips.

Embedded Weblinks
Gain additional information for research.

Try This!
Complete activities and hands-on experiments.

WHAT'S ONLINE?

Try This!	**Embedded Weblinks**	**Video**	**EXTRA FEATURES**
Test your knowledge of important events in African American sports history.	Find out more about the history of African Americans in sports.	Watch a video about African Americans in sports.	**Audio** Listen to sections of the book read aloud.
Write a biography about a notable African American athlete.	Learn more about notable people from *Great African Americans–Sports*.	Watch a video about a notable moment of African Americans in sports.	**Key Words** Study vocabulary, and complete a matching word activity.
Create a timeline of important events in an African American athlete's life.	Link to more notable achievements of African Americans in sports.		
Complete a writing activity about an important topic in the book.			**Slide Show** View images and captions, and prepare a presentation.
Design your own trophy for African American athletes.			**Quizzes** Test your knowledge.

AV² was built to bridge the gap between print and digital. We encourage you to tell us what you like and what you want to see in the future.
Sign up to be an AV² Ambassador at www.av2books.com/ambassador.